Last Red Dirt Embrace

Last Red Dirt Embrace

W.K. Stratton

LITERARY PRESS
LAMAR UNIVERSITY

ISBN: 978-1-942956-00-6
Library of Congress Control Number: 2022944763

Manufactured in the USA

Lamar University Literary Press
Beaumont, Texas

To the memory of Fred Bross and Richard Reed

Recent Poetry from Lamar University Literary Press

Lisa Adams, *xuai: mission, house, village, town*
Bobby Aldridge, *An Affair of the Stilled Heart*
Michael Baldwin, *Lone Star Heart, Poems of a Life in Texas*
Walter Bargen, *My Other Mother's Red Mercedes*
Christine Boldt, *For Every Tatter*
David Bowles, *Flower, Song, Dance: Aztec and Mayan Poetry*
Jerry Bradley, *Collapsing into Possibility*
Jerry Bradley, *Crownfeathers and Effigies*
Jerry Bradley and Ulf Kirchdorfer, editors, *The Great American Wise Ass Poetry Anthology*
Matthew Brennan, *One Life*
Mark Busby, *Through Our Times*
Julie Chappell, *Mad Habits of a Life*
Stan Crawford, Resisting Gravity
Chip Dameron, *Waiting for an Etcher*
Glover Davis, *My Mad Cap of Darkness*
William Virgil Davis, *The Bones Poems*
Jeffrey DeLotto, *Voices Writ in Sand*
Chris Ellery, *Elder Tree*
Dede Fox, *On Wings of Silence*
Alan Gann, *That's Entertainment*
Katherine Hoerth, *Goddess Wears Cowboy Boots*
Katherine Hoerth, *Odes and Elegies: Eco-Poetry from the Texas Gulf Coast*
Michael Jennings, *Crossings, a Record of Travel*
Betsy Joseph, *Only So Many Autumns*
Lynn Hoggard, *First Light*
Lynn Hoggard, *Motherland*
Michale Jennings, *Crossings: a Record of Travel*
Ulf Kirchdorfer, *Chewing Green Leaves*
Ulf Kirchdorfer, *Hamlet in Exile*
Laozi, *Daodejing*, tr. By David Breeden, Steven Schroeder, and Wally Swist
Janet McCann, *The Crone at the Casino*
Jim McGarrah, *A Balancing Act*
Laurence Musgrove, *Local Bird*
Benjamin Myers, *Black Sunday*
Janice Northerns, *Some Electric Hum*
Godspower Oboido, *Wandering Feet on Pebbled Shores*
Dave Oliphant, The Pilgrimage, Selected Poems: 1962-2012
Carol Coffee Reposa, *Underground Musicians*
Jan Seale, *A Lifetime of Words*
Jan Seale, *The Parkinson Poems*
Jan Seale, *Particulars*
Glen Sorestad *Hazards of Eden*
Vincent Spina, *The Sumptuous Hills of Gulfport*
W.K. Stratton, *Betrayal Creek*
W.K. Stratton, *Colo-State-Pen: 18456, a dark Miscellany*
W.K. Stratton, *Ranchero Ford/ Dying in Red Dirt Country*
Gary Swaim, *Quixotic Notions*
Waldman, Ken, *Sports Page*
Loretta Diane Walker, *Desert Light*
Loretta Diane Walker, *Ode to My Mother's Voice*
Dan Williams, *Past Purgatory, a Distant Paradise*
Dan Williams, *Yet at the Gates, a Refuge of Sunflowers and Milkweed*
Jonas Zdanys, *The Angled Road*
Jonas Zdanys (ed.), *Pushing the Envelope, Epistolary Poems*
Jonas Zdanys, *Red Stones*
Jonas Zdanys, *Three White Horses*

For information on these and other Lamar University Literary Press books go to
www.Lamar.edu/literarypress

And how Death is that remedy all singers dream of, sing, remember,
    prophesy as in the Hebrew Anthem, or the Buddhist Book of
Answers—
    and my own imagination of a withered leaf—at dawn—
Dreaming back thru life, Your time—and mine accelerating toward
    Apocalypse,
the final moment—the flower burning in the Day—and what comes
    after . . . like a poem in the dark
                    —Allen Ginsberg, *Kaddish*

Cela est bien dit, répondit Candide, mais il faut cultiver notre jardin.
                    —Voltaire, *Candide, ou L'optimisme*

The *Dreaming Sam Peckinpah Quintet*

Dreaming Sam Peckinpah, Ink Brush Press,
Betrayal Creek, Lamar University Literary Press
Colo-State-Pen: 18456, a Dark Miscellany, Lamar U. Press
Ranchero Ford/ Dying in Red Dirt Country, Lamar U. Press
Last Red Dirt Embrace, Lamar U. Press

Preface

At some point in the mid 1970s, I acquired a skinny book called *Outlyer and Ghazals* by Jim Harrison. I was an undergraduate from nowhere attending a nowhere college. I was three-quarters ignorant. I didn't know Jim Harrison from William Henry Harrison. And I didn't know a ghazal from a gazelle. I think I'd seen a gazelle at the Oklahoma City Zoo. I later crossed paths with Harrison twice, once in Livingston and once in Austin. I enjoyed brief conversations with him.

Now I know what a ghazal is. I know what follows does not constitute a collection of ghazals. In fact, it is a single long poem. But the way I structured the numbered stanzas is influenced by Harrison's experiments with the form and how he used language and, particularly, enjambment in that book. It made me think about verse horizontally instead of vertically. Harrison broke a lot of rules and created new forms. I'm sorry he no longer walks among us. I think he was a great poet and fiction writer.

I'm not Jewish. I was raised as a Campbellite, Disciples of Christ variant. Nowadays I refer to myself as a Taoist Cowboy. In places I respectfully borrow the word Kaddish, in particular in reference to the "Mourners Kaddish," from Jewish religious tradition. I first became acquainted with the term through Allen Ginsberg's *Kaddish*, which of course is verse mourning his mother. It is among his best work. *Kaddish*, in part, inspired what follows, which concerns the death of my mother. I should state that the mother appearing in these lines is both my mother but also a metaphor. For the most part, these stanzas were written in journal style on my iPad.

WKS

1.

I roll my mother's final garden hoses. Red tail hawks
Overhead weep and celebrate. Clouds dissolve the sun.

I hear a train two miles away. This was Comancheria.
Now I guide people to used trailer houses for sale.

Form resolves nothing. I am alone and walls are brown.
Grasslands beyond doors are the most challenging.

I used to leave a woman's house at Sunday noon. Cities
Embrace careless lovers. I'm a scalp hunter in her mind.

Today I run in coyote country where I was born. My step-
Brother and I broker death. For once we share our blood.

2.

Viral tyranny. My mother is deposited with the lost.
I know where I shall bury her. Roadrunners hunt snakes

In that graveyard. Empoisoned moles somehow thrive
Among headstones. They drill soda-can-width tunnels

And kick up dirt pyramids on winterkill grass. They own
No passion for gophers. My stepfather flew me across

Rooms with the back of his hand, kicked me with size 12
Boots. My mother nestled him. I was instructed to love Jesus.

He awaits Mom in red dirt cradle, shrew shaft surrounded.
I am disconnected. I respect only low-lying outlaw tombs.

3.

I recollect a night when Gene Lehmann and I shot pool
At a short-lived pizzeria not far from the nursing home.

Someone played Wings' "Nineteen Hundred and Eighty-Five"
On the jukebox as we took money off three Chickasaw guys.

Pizza storefront is boarded up tonight. Nursing home thrives.
Back then Sir Paul lamented not getting enough sweet stuff.

Gene and I: hellbent nine-ball demons. Mom never sensed
I owned slick concrete tastes for speed and red dirt weed.

Wings was a terrible band, McCartney, less said the better.
At midnight I rode bareback paint across short grass plains.

4.

Toothless woman – Need Help cardboard sign – reclining
On the satin of asphalt, motorhomes passing, no beer.

I remember her as I speak to my mother on the phone.
Mirror soap scummed, I cannot shave, paint a spirit.

She does not eat shrimp: hives. She does not work.
She smells everything. The moon breaks her nose.

Smoking room, only thing available. Yellow Page love
Only kind available. Cold water, diesel air: also available.

I recall anxiety outside Cheyenne. Little America pushed
Me through. Sixteen days now, headache gone, waiting.

5.

I failed South Dakota. I remember old Bill Ramsey's
Carolina Quarterly words: Ride the American theme.

Someday, he said, you will be a necessary poet.
How can I respond? I disregarded Belle Fourche.

My pickup wheels need replacing. This is unsafe.
My mother rode a bus through these badlands.

Pregnant and sleeping on the ground crushed her.
Through her skin I drew Dakota earth and tears.

Bill Ramsey suggested I read Jack Kerouac. Sigh.
I knew more highways. This one rolls onward.

6.

Shame is outdoor breath in October on the plains.
Even as a child I never liked my mother to touch me.

I cannot feel satisfied about that. I pushed her away.
Steam cocoons my face as I huff through gray days.

My mother disdained Mexicans. To her they were dirty.
Ice edged her stock tank. She failed to embrace grammar.

I recall her hawking phlegm into blue willow cups.
Later she extinguished cigarettes in coffee-spit messes.

Mom slipped on water at the nursing home last night.
I count Greyhound Lines at Oklahoma City station.

7.

Five a.m. glares harsh in bathroom light.
I ponder what love can define. I am a cowboy.

We do not speak of such things. I violate code
Even mouthing this. Assignation among us

Is contradiction, blossom against hailstone.
I unpeel leather chaps and store lariats.

Loving self is a prairie tornado unwinding.
Horizons gape. Fleeing feels effortless.

My mother chased barn shards at twenty.
She knew storm winds, barbwire shrapnel.

8.

I am 1/128th Cherokee. I decline the disrespect
The senator embraced. Like her I am a white person.

Fractions do not register, never mind Dawes Commission
Entries and intrigues. Mom accepted family fabrication.

She claimed I am a warrior's grandson. Relative sighs.
Outside a squirrel limps from one tree to another.

I saw two kinds of owls during last night's stroll.
My skin was a perch belly in cold moonlight.

My mother is expiring in colostomy stench.
I fail the art of uncovering and mourning.

9.

Spilled mezcal on flat rocks and expiring grass,
Jan Reid's share in our toasting his legacies.

We are masked and distanced, as required.
Dick, David, and I speak of Big Bend burro roping.

Mom suffered through a bad night and morning.
Nurse says she shows no signs of being Active.

"Active" — last switch to turn in dying schematic.
Irony lines breathing's conduits and sewage pipes.

I eat carnitas y tortillas de maíz. I watch the sun.
I have lived here a thousand years. I am a child.

10.

Comanche walking stick in the corner becomes
Western diamondback fangs bare, venom trailing.

I look again, see only a cow skull residing
On wood and steel beneath east windows.

It followed me down Wichita Mountains trail:
God transformed into granite faces in the sun.

I never shared this with my mother. She confused
Sacred places with Disciples of Christ cinderblocks.

No in thunder, I recollect such words spray-painted on
1950s Studebakers at First Christian prayer houses.

11.

Horse lot across from West Side house never retires.
Grandpa's skin is the color of an aging saddle. Eyes

Like coffee brewed too long. Old Bill's never painted
House blasted to nickels by sun, wind unrelenting.

Red dust devils swirl among hungry mares at dawn.
I own no gift for clemency. Mom is the same way.

Grandma confessed Mom gave her just one bad year.
I trudge this earth because of it. Clouded full moon —

Fred and I recited rustic Amidah over red dirt and
Johnson grass beyond hog pens we built ourselves.

12.

Standing prayer this morning outside my boxing gym.
Kaddish for Fred: May his great name be sanctified.

Father of night: we strolled through cicada acrimony
And thumped scorpions from hay bales in real church.

The One is that which can never be Biblically nailed.
To corral it is to release it among plains buffalo at dawn.

Boyd Elder gave DeGueren Texas bison skull petrified,
True saint and martyr remnant. Sparring regenerates.

Mom wept when Fred died. She fashioned tithes. Here is
A secret she hid away: Dad was a bulldogger, not a rider.

13.

Photos in cobwebs and boxed disdain. Fred and I
Aged fourteen, bad haircuts, Kodak Brownie crinkles.

First Christian souvenirs from Mom's Sunday School.
She taught while secretly pregnant with me. Flood bottom

Thick with cottonwood and honey locust, thorns at risk.
Another photo of Fred: High school, color fading, haircut

Even worse. Mom suffered two nursing home falls this week.
Fred and I warred against ticks, red cedar, hoof and mouth.

Plains ice storm before Halloween. Power lines, trees ruined.
I am the supplicant of crow and vulture cathedrals.

14.

Fred and I were rough lumber, failed sandstone walls.
Where does a Dog Soldier gallop in this empty dark?

After hay hauling we stripped and reclined on sand
To permit Cimarron salt to absolve scorpion grievance.

Pawnee pow-wows in Verdigris sun. Frybread nights in town.
Beaded Ponca warbonnet mirror hanging by monofilament.

Mom enjoyed Indian dances if lodges were not too dirty.
She ranged that way during rodeo days, white shirt stained.

Surrender, betrayal: stones in dented five gallon can.
Lawnmower hums in the distance, leaf blower demise.

15.

John Trudell afternoon. Crows follow dawn.
Homecoming will not be long. Frosted grass.

Little things embed. If Waylon Jennings needed
Money he headed to Na-Diné to perform.

Awe struck Navajos like straws in a cigar box.
Waylon leather bound. Mooney, complex DNA.

I attended Diné rodeos. In dreams I was enemy:
Comanche. I required ceremony, smoke, light.

My mother vomits this week, despises her Depends.
Recovery is Rainy Mountain, the Medicine Mounds.

16.

Pre-dawn Oklahoma: I watch *Wanted: Dead or Alive*,
Everything leaden and alive in McQueen's eyes. Mom

And I saw him in *Junior Bonner* the last time we went
To the movies together: my favorite Peckinpah picture

Because it is my story, her story, a thousand convolutions.
Fog as gray as McQueen's 1950s television skin settles in.

I am road weary and Marty Stuart-overdosed this morning.
I could have been an Old West dishonest keno dealer.

My past is future. Never been this tired. Or so awake.
I contemplate ghosts, tattoos, and habanero salsa.

17.

Return to saguaro highway. Last night: Arizona Motel.
Promises I would never roll down this route again.

I know pentas back home are iced over, Egyptian
Stars the color of my dying mother's teeth and skin.

She complained about New Mexico Mescalero police
When driving to Las Vegas bowling tournaments.

My parents owned Continentals they could not afford.
I remember free range Apache cowboys herding cattle.

I was fourteen and collected grasshopper extremities.
Black angus flooded the canyon. I saddled a new horse.

18.

Tonight I watch *Run, Angel, Run!* starring William Smith.
Jack Starrett directed: Gulf flatlands soldered to his eyes.

Jan met him in San Marcos on *A Small Town in Texas*.
Starrett was an asshole, he said, but smart, very smart.

Flash on him in *Kid Blue*: Delightful sadist bleeding out.
His portrait: absorbed actor, competency clawing director.

Night insects dissolve like soap flakes in boiling water:
That time of year. My mother loathed biker flick hoods.

She outlived Starrett by thirty years. Cleft rocks of ages.
Washer empties, dryer mantra. Hot wind and switchgrass.

19.

Nursing home falls abide. Now we transport my mother
To safety zones. I see her again via plexiglass night sweats.

I read Hemingway for the first time in years, Pamplona filtered
Through Oklahoma red dirt. I am nothing remarkable. Often

Death is a sweet lover's greeting kiss and deposits shadows
And hoists sparks. I own no more words to tell my mother.

I have pondered unbridged rivers for sixty-five years and more.
I am beyond reconciliations. I race Interstate 35 again.

I regret each spotlight I shined on myself. I failed my mother
When she was afraid, heeding empty lover demands instead.

20.

I wasted love and stout nylon rope on convocation
I could never claim or even reflect. I am driving now:

Fort Worth, a place that owned and discharged me.
I received baptism in Disciples of Christ bricks and glass

Two hundred twenty-eight miles due north of here.
I suffered strep throat and sin where I-30 and I-35

Crossbreed in asphalt, concrete, steel. Now I am healed.
My mother walked First Christian paths. Can she recall?

No time now for any poised purpose. *I shall not miss her.*
There. It is stated. Am I monster or realist? Both, both.

21.

A year ago I ordered a rebozo from Oaxaca.
I spent many hours and many dollars on it.

Valueless as recycled supermarket plastic sacks:
She received it that way during betrayal sagas.

That woman was unknown to my mother. Squandered
Romance in vapid South Austin suburbs, I am unbound

Yet still incarcerated in those hollow habitations.
My mother will die before Christmas. The betrayer

Parties with shredded screens and claw-ripped furniture.
She will never value clean textile or blue agave spirit.

22.

Fred dealt ditch weed and became Libertarian.
He wanted no safety net except himself. I understand.

My mother mouthed such notions as self-dependence.
She grew cabbage, squash, okra, corn. She painted oils.

My parents believed failure tattooed itself on my brow.
But I learned to break horses and grew into a warrior.

On the broiling Llano Estacado I forsook my white eyes.
Her son's survival astonished Mom. I saved my parents

From bankruptcy and grew as unpliable as buffalo horn.
Norther howls. I miss Fred. Cedar elms are leafless.

23.

My mother tells me she aches from this life's shadows.
She believes in celestial shores and Jesus floodlights.

I wish her amity of flight. Her tombstone awaits, missing
Only a date. I deal my karma from a deck with no wild cards.

I understand goodbye and hello are synonyms. Blue skies fail.
I require grieving. Fire ants raise dirt among Mexican petunias.

I cup mound soil and massage it into my face. I feel nothing.
I am an uncircumcised gentile. Kaddish is foreign landscape.

I ask for abundant peace, amen, but my eyes remain parched.
Mirrors reveal insect venom welts exploding my cheeks.

24.

Thanksgiving means nothing more than roadkill smear
On freezing asphalt between Gotebo and Mountain View.

Two buzzards mount telephone poles to holiday feast.
My mother baked dressing with oysters. Only I devoured it.

Those decades fall behind me now. I learn of wheelchair demise
At memory care. I listen. I store away. I own too many journeys.

Highway silence is thunder rolling. I retain nothing, everything.
My mother will die in twenty days. I spot a grassfire to the east.

I recollect call to service. Flames bit my elbows. I attempted
Hose magic. It worked. I am here: two hundred miles to drive.

25.

Postal Service item in possession: How can I relay
How much I hated McCartney and Wings in the day?

My mother is a locust husk hugging the garage door.
I recollect an album that appeared in 1975, the year

She turned forty, terrible shit, but I listened to
Letting Go till it tickled every submerged gray urge

I ever possessed. Owls begin evening's dirge. I do
Feel like letting go. My time has become concession

Diseased. Cats and rabbits shall perish by night talons:
Blood and fur splotches on morning sun concrete.

26.

I grieve by wrapping pipes six weeks ahead of freezes.
I ensure right corral fencing before horses gallop in.

Today: nursing home/undertaker/preacher conversations.
God is grasshopper tobacco juice and discarded lover moans.

I listen to an ancient hymn: No Expectations, the Rolling Stones.
Brian Jones' slide is every lamentation I have ever uttered.

No one should face mom's exit. Denver Peckinpah drove
His dying dog to the country and fed it sirloin. After loving pats

And final goodbyes, he shot it in the head. That is dignity.
That is respect. Rain dulled morning and I resist all road calls.

27.

Tynan's truth: we seek teeth to match our wounds.
I sort incisors, canines, and tusks for enamel razors

Corresponding to martyred skin. I find nothing that fits.
I never met anyone's needs, least of all my own. I passed

Through my mother. I am not of her. Gibbous moon pale
As my lips climbs the east sky. I do not mean to affront.

My mother spoke endlessly about me. I became her badge.
I cannot say if she is alive at this moment. I feel wind shifts.

I hope I am not Tommy Lee Jones in lunatic overdrive, fury
And threat. I can say I am human. Nothing less or more.

28.

Two whistling ducks pass the night on roof ridge. I see them
In dull gray light. I await a demise update. Hunger is foreign.

Yesterday I triggered a shotgun for the first time in three decades.
My shoulder is recoil sore. My mother was twenty-four before

She learned to shoot. I never once saw her dance. She liked to bowl.
She possessed no voice for singing. Poise jilted her as did happiness.

I hear ash leaves slamming concrete. Blake taught us that God
Created both tiger and lamb. He was wrong. They made Him.

I had to be born through my mother. She was the only highway.
Sheriff is drunk and calls me. He cries for Mom. He is dying too.

29.

I read Mailer often, cancer as metaphor and reality.
My mother's pent-up tumors exploded without portent.

Four months later and I am still in disbelief. I return to
A Patti Smith book I should have destroyed. Her sentences

Form, inform, reform. Cold rain this dawn. I love Patti Smith.
I withhold bridge construction. I am warned traffic will not

Match expectation. I record Patti Smith reciting Blake.
My mother saw her on television once: She's ugly, can't sing:

Mom's scowled dismissals. So familiar. Patti Smith sings better
Than anyone. She exudes beauty. She wears a surfer's cross.

30.

My mother read a book a week for seventy-five years.
I learned the comfort of pages in hand from her.

She poached eggs with black pepper and vinegar hints
And served them with salsa picante and biscuits.

It was glory I will miss. Now I slay bathtub silverfish. Zen
Fails me at such tasks. For all the books she devoured

My mother never knew Gwendolyn Brooks or James Welch.
She was ignorant of Blake and Mailer. Patti Smith's words

Meant nothing to her. She liked cozy crimes by kilted men.
Dead cedar elm leaves invade this space. I own no brooms.

31.

New day and I wake in both Texas and Utah. Before dawn
I confront Arches and snake hiss Brushy Creek alike. Highway

Traffic roar always the same, tinnitus of semi-trailer trucks.
My mother hated mornings. She demanded coffee black

And inked news on paper. Ancient motel bed unyielding
Seventeen minutes from Temple Square. Mattress at home

Even worse. It is best to sleep alone. My mother lauded
Mormon ancestors. She understood nothing of the faith.

She thought Presbyterians embraced strange views. She lies
Swaddled in her own piss and shit at daybreak: our destiny.

32.

Post Dwight Yoakam concert haze in 1990s recollection:
Hotel romp with brunette whose name I never learned

Or forgot a month later. I understand these machinations.
My mother was the same in mid-1950s — only different

Music, state, town, motel double bed, hombre — I cannot
Condemn her for being what I am. We both dismissed truths

Like insecticide-soaked yellow jacket nests. I loathed her lies
As I hammered my mirrored face into flowerbed gravel.

She was afraid and owned no options. Kitchen ant invasion
At midnight — I sit in darkness. We never really connected.

33.

Sleeping too many nights at my mother's house, torture bed
Too short, too unyielding, maybe four bathroom piss trips

Between midnight and dawn — it is never like this elsewhere.
Outside — the fine and deadly snow invitation. All is hushed.

Six a.m. coffee. Piled invoices and receipts on dining room table
Are drifts filling sandstone crevices along the Cimarron River.

Comanche disdain owls perching on headboard above me.
My mother's people slew redtail hawks, owls too: instinct.

I am free and enslaved here: cougar pacing zoo dwellings.
Bang a gong/act naturally, nothing soothes. Dying persists.

34.

Woman leaves me because she hates boxing. Response? I tattoo
Cleto Reyes Hecho en Mexico logo on my right calf. My mother

Didn't understand my ring desire. Wrestling, yes. Grandpa
Obsessed it. His face was a first baseman's mitt. But I never

Once knew him to watch a single inning. Eagle alighted in tree
Across the street, cavalier cat threat as tall as my shin.

Mom mistook eagles for crows, subscribed to pious toads.
She felt no loss until I moved away. She fell, helpless.

I can't know what to claim. I loathe cold inoculation.
Mom never knew my ink. I kept much hidden: rattler in leaves.

35.

Home again. Pocket gopher works lantana beds at dawn.
Thirty degrees, holidays edge closer, my mother's soul

Invades Geomyidae fur. I own claw carved rodent tunnels.
Grub subsistence: I burrowed through darkness for decades,

Incisors tobacco yellow though I never smoked. Nighttime
Whiskers like bleached dead sunrays. Dirt tubes sheltered me

From owl talons and the fists and boots of my stepfather. Cancer
Announced itself then sentenced my mother to ninety days.

No surprise: Insecticides, defoliants, solvents, diesel flatulence,
Denial were her daily bread. Underground eyes ache for light.

36.

I muse on how Jack Starrett might direct these scenes. He owned
Style, not great, but serviceable. He maintained no Refugio love.

I ordered *Mr. Horn* from Alabama bootleggers, TV capture with
Static in doublewide moldering. Frayed David Carradine images,

Pelicula herida yet I can see Starrett's stamp. He foresaw our
Present: excellence equals nothing, just get the job finished.

My friend Woody encounters rattlesnakes in his trailer house.
He leaves his door open to invite invasion. I know that Zen.

Thunder of almost winter wakes me at 5 a.m. My mother
Could not comprehend Starrett or Woody nor that sacristy.

37.

Home is not home: absent while present, tyranny of 4:45 a.m.
I ponder anole eggs abandoned in frozen Texas gumbo.

My dewlap and dorsal ridge expand. Black spots behind eyes
Intensify. I sense invaders yet cannot move. I am cold-blooded.

My mother lowered me to lizard level. She stood overhead.
I shed skins and forsook my tail. Green blood skinks abounded,

Brother killers, soul cannibals. She placed me on wheat altars.
All in the past, I survived, burrowing into active reptile earth.

My mother soon rejoins the red dirt whence she leapt. I know
No dirges. Sun cracks darkest morning/night. I shiver and wait.

38.

Ray Wylie Hubbard sings about New Braunfels Snake Farm
And interstate whorehouse: Turn right and women waited

For dads in travel trailers. Go left, sons in pit viper pursuit.
Dee Dee Ramone fancied 1970s Snake Farm t-shirts: history

Ancient. Mother never had a clue. She knew rodeo backseats
And lakeside Pink Elephant beer joints. Before her mind fled

She told me about oilfield boyfriends, workover rig madness,
Including a driller I worked for. She hated Hank Williams

Whose songs reminded her of too many inherited blisters.
I ponder buying Biff Davis saddles: morning breaks too bright.

39.

I scrub my face at my mother's house. Hair wet, unshaved, I roll
Toward nursing home obligation. Elden and I enter plexiglass

Pandemic protection. America is intubated. Politicians ooze into
Every cranny, zombie culture, Kardashian horror, world rusted.

Elden: overalls, bulldozer cap, swollen, fractured
From Vietnam 50 years ago, owns his shit now, ¡que milagro!

"Charlie don't surf" is a favorite movie line. Mom now appears
In wheelchair. Kolaches confuse her. She cannot manage tea.

She says she wants sleep. We will never see her alive again. Cold
Street and Elden says he won't die this way. I accept this.

40.

My mother's unknotting is my own. I see where I will be
In twenty years. We all collapse. We all reassemble.

I dread my unmasking and return by bloody birth canal,
Light and dark, dark and light never ending. Chanting

Drone and desired memory of galloping Comanche horses
Stolen from Spain onto sunblasted Llano Estacado. I ride

In loincloth and medicine paint and honesty. My dying
Occurs beneath Apache stone war club with brain splash

And honor. My mother expires in plastic disinfectant and
Big Pharma outrage. It is sin. She screeches day and night.

41.

Clear day with a sunset of cherry candy and orange peels,
Now a half moon preens above my dinted pickup truck.

My mother is nursing home pinned near Cross Timbers.
I dream a gourd dance with Comanche friends. Hear me:

I once fantasized the tallest of the Medicine Mounds.
Noble man breathed into an eagle bone whistle at night.

White bird the size of a fire hydrant stood on caliche
Clawing its way up the plains dome at cinnamon dawn.

I failed Revelations and tractor repair school demands
But understood those spaces. I prepared for home.

42.

My mother fancied me a preacher: Hushpuppy shoes,
Polyester pants and shirt, clip on tie, Disciples of Christ

Cream of wheat without end, amen. I strayed to beer joint
Liturgies and Oakland Raider metaphysics instead, failing

Calls to minister to old women in nursing homes while
Rifling their pocketbooks for cash: clergy's primary skill.

I read D.H. Lawrence, first time in decades, holiness
In Nottingham coal mine words — Ursula Brangwen:

Aching for passion in lockstep binary world. I seek it too.
My mother is abandoned barns and silos. I am prairie fire.

43.

Kin of mine heard Saint Buriana in Cornwall oratory.
She preached to my Lizard Point people not far from

Cruk Trefyffian. Grandparents' deposited skulls worn
To dust among Stone Dance relics — I know fogous and

Iron: Meaningless across ocean and continent yet
Etched on my palms and eyebrows. I grasp the core:

I am nothing. You are nothing. The universe is nothing.
My mother, nothing. Only One exists. By writing this

I diminish it. Sam Peckinpah understood. He filmed his
Western in St Bruyan, same as Tombstone/Dodge City.

44.

Holiness is flesh, sweat, and twisted bedsheet sacristy.
It cannot reside in basilica ceiling paint or brush arbor.

Yet it also can — lotus legs. My mother sought solace
From TV preachers and thin tracts. She believed paradise

Lies in her clouds. I hope she found peace in that faith.
She screams bound behind pandemic walls and doors.

In her house I find wedding ring receipt, a purchase
She made unmarried and five months pregnant with me:

Another mystery never solved. I rewatch *The Gunfighter*.
Perhaps Mom shot her son to kill pain. Prairie sleet falls.

45.

I surrendered explanations long ago. Deliverance
Equated nothing, only squirrel barks against muddy

Lovers lanes and Highland Park black box theater.
My youth is faded, torn, creased Fogarty Junior High

Stage backdrop of forests that never existed. Mom
Liked to see me act in plays. I preferred imploding

Red ant dens with cherry bombs. I tore grasshopper
Legs to conjure anguish. Elden once torched a hayfield.

Dale fled Guthrie, an abandoned dog never rescued,
No forever home. Our childhood: crushed Easter eggs.

46.

I carry gut scars and distended muscle decline. No repair
Possible: Unmasked physician eyes aim directly at mine.

She is tall, gloved, at ease in lab coat. Surgical light
Glows from clear forehead and hair the color of night.

She is all my mother never could be. Deception remains
A torn, putrid, incomplete quilt encasing old woman

Flesh and soul, hideous baby blanket never released.
More than once she tried to suffocate me with it. I am

Exposed now, tube injected in penis, my core visible
On adjacent screen. I'm sorry, doctor says and sighs.

47.

Greenland sharks adapt to prairie ways and I am one. I promote
My dentition and lethal flesh. I measure twenty-one feet. I was

Born in 1620. I knew Comanche as farmers. I paddled against
American buffalo herds numbering six million. Little Turtle

Tapped my spirit against St. Clair. I warned of falling timbers,
No avail. He said I lacked woodland insight. My mother never

Trusted me. Her husband rejected my post-surgery offerings.
He said I was deficient. He called for my stepbrother. I swam

Oklahoma City asphalt currents, subsisted on plankton and
Roadkill, no hospital backward glances. I am alive and deadly.

48.

Faith of our fathers, these rocks cleave for thee, unbroken
Circles — we all fly away, amen, and river gather beneath

Bloodied sunrises. My sanity is flimsy: paper hosts baked
By nuns cloistered on Oklahoma City back alleys. These are

Bodies of Donald Trump and Christ transubstantiated.
I no longer own weapons but understand: To walk safely

Through valleys of the shadow of death you must possess
Three-inch magnum twelve-gauge outrage. I confide all.

My mother's religion is black-and-white static minus liturgy
Froth. She is near dead. I disconnect and smell night skunks.

49.

Thanksgiving arrives in peace through betrayal, sacred turkey
Microwave enhanced. I miss Cheyenne friends. I recall nine-ball

In beer joint sacristy, Conway Twitty fleeing jukebox lockdown,
Parking lot weed and coke deals, unveiled 1970s liberation but

Shatter of confidence, no matter, highway miles always heal,
And I think of HL listening to Neil Young *Decade* vinyl ancient

And far away: I loved and love her in ways only we can fathom,
Wichita Falls cyclone survival, collecting my worst yet pushing

Onward through insanity edifice and red dirt dusk. My mother
Never knew her. I read D.H. Lawrence before blank TV screens.

50.

Now and always, December 1, 2020 — Austin sunny
And I enter four-lanes, wired on truck stop coffee

And regret, grasping for movie last scenes. How would
Peckinpah shoot this? What tricks would Lucien Ballard

Unreel? Give me Holden's two-word line and Robards'
Acceptance. L.Q. Jones skulks in black across Durango

Roof: *Us old boys oughtn't to be doing this to each other.* . .
No: not in cinema, not in real life. Usual stops in Texas

Czech land, FaceTime goodbye plan in place, Oklahoma
In darkness, then the call, Mrs. Waner just died: fadeout.

51.

And so: pipeline rupture, last shared joint to snowy
November day/Benedictine nuns punching keys

In hospital accounting rooms/real doctor gone fishing
Or playing poker or both/sky government soul gray/

Byron Berline's father-in-law steps in with impromptu
Deliverance on Hospital Hill/habit sisters present invoice

For sixty dollars/circumcision five dollars extra/luxury
Beyond means/Mom, broke/Grandma presents three

Jackson-faced crumpled bills/coffee can currency
Hidden away from Grandpa/red dirt shame ascends.

52.

My mother's house, sometime past midnight, television
On *Man from Del Rio*, journey to grays and shadowland,

Manuel Antonio Rodolfo Quinn Oaxaca y María Cristina
Estela Marcela Jurado García — Anthony Quinn, Katy

Jurado — two native Mexicans top-billed in Western
Melody Ranch filmed as I first breathed and forced

Open my eyes, played Guthrie's State theater while I
Nursed horseflies and mystery in red dust twilight.

I study the gem Jurado. Mom lies on mortuary metal.
She was my unfinished highway. I hear Oklahoma wind.

53.

No sleep follows *Man from Del Rio* — just tequila
And the dark. Billy Joe Shaver's "Thunderbird" streams

Time and again. My mother's handwritten attempt at
Memoir collapses after eleven pages. She specialized

In dangled lists and lives. For years it was my saddle burr.
I serenade her in indecent Spanish about swallow flight.

She'd know this tune: Bob Wills and Elvis both rendered
It on corrupt vinyl. BJS hurrahs lust and cheap wine

As I sing of farewell. Now: "Canción Mixteca," out of key
With myself, no trills, drunk, and sleepless — all I can do.

54.

Dawn blues: mother protector never showed up. Brothers
But not brothers endured bite of straightened wire hangers

On bare legs, blood rivulets hell bound: she nodded and
And watched wide-eyed. Same for size 12 punts over hedge

And rosebush. I cowered beneath trailer house beds unable
To stop shaking. Straighten up, fly right if you do not like it:

Her words. Oklahoma wind whipped plains and waving wheat
That smelled not sweet but like sour mash. I worked harvests.

Faded Polaroid and legal document memories in this house:
No passes for my crimes, just poison springs marker trees.

55.

Morning in this house unhaunted: funeral plans placed,
Ancient George Harrison tune reverberates dark end

Cloud 9. Why? I cannot say. I fail Tao. I encompass Tao —
Gloves, loves, messes, pieces. I kissed my mother in hospital

Fluorescence and said I loved her. I did not lie — last time
I touched her alive. Mortuary delivery of her final clothes

In an hour. December heater begins its roar. I hear backhoe
Red dirt work in next door cemetery. Death is life rebooted.

Pandemic masks and black death carts, bells ringing always,
Cowboy drums leading Old West TB coffins: I've been there.

56.

I deposit her clothes. Cloud 9 pulses in silence. Casket
Color contracted, brief rain — I pay dead woman's bills

While vested in ancient denim and 1970s Waylon Jennings
Concert t-shirt, not fitting attire for prairie graveside

Service in two days. Mom loved Conway Twitty, Mac Davis,
And Elvis. She thought Waylon looked like a thug, her word,

And his phase shifted guitar sounded broken. She was born
Two years ahead of him. She was a century older. Waylon was

Cocaine, Hells Angels, diesel, big voice highway freedom.
I set off for Texas for tie, untorn jeans, shined funeral boots.

57.

Dark I-35 miles and I listen to Lightnin' Hopkins, Hank,
Lydia Mendoza, and Waylon live shots from 1974 —

Dallas Western Palace, Austin Texas Opry House, about
The time I left high school — rocky DNA, still birth blind,

Natural rambler, maybe the bad man of Mendoza's song,
Coal chunk, no diamond potential, red dirt instructions.

Clatter in midnight dark house: Light reveals panicked
Wren — Mom's favorite bird — in living room, terror

Heart visible. I am sorry, I say, and flush her through door.
You can't stay here. She shoots straight into low cloud night.

58.

Trust no one, reject sweet potatoes, decline flight patterns,
Running never resolved anything, memorized lines etched

Against two hours of sleep — this highway always demands
More than I can bestow. Now dead grass field in shaded

Morning light, collapsed prefabs rusting, diesel engine
Cacophony along scrapyard wastelands, the road, the road,

The road, no escape, back to Oklahoma yet again, my mother
Drained and stiff in mortuary tedium of gray and blue, goodbyes

To come. I died six times before birth. Mom never held that.
Her life was *As the World Turns* in black-and-white shadowland.

59.

I shall not sleep again in that house — highway hotel
In frozen night, sprayed and masked, my hometown

Enforces no engine braking prohibition: diesel screams
Shatter parked car frost and my dreams. I am unarmed.

I forsook family bleached blood privilege at this place.
Now I am required to say Kaddish for my dead mother.

I will repeat it for eleven months. I am the good son. I am
The worst. I reject community. I loathe inner scrutiny.

But I am of a ten-cowboy minyan who gather to recite
The redneck Torah. My grief path is crooked, icebound.

60.

Celebrity politicians, programmed music, prescribed language,
Our reality TV show America: my mother's back patio devolved

Into freeze-killed tomato vines, smashed ceramics, forsaken
Brooms and loppers, and centers never solid. Funeral Friday

And gravesites are obscured by bulldozed dead tree mountains,
No easy cemetery parking. Impatient preachers play video games

On iPhones. Elden and I viewed her embalmed in casket yawn,
Transformed into Grandma Effie, whom she never resembled

While breathing. I am as detached as snake hunter roadrunners
Down the way. Ranch trucks roll past this last red dirt embrace.

61.

Roadrunners and moles are our prophets. They comprehend
Our condemned fate. I crave snake hunting wisdom. I require

Light of blind tunnels. At cemetery gate my phone buzzes:
Bootmaker Armando in Raymondville says my new bull hides

Are ready to ship, leathers of peanut butter and spring grass,
Riding heels and shafts fang-proof elevated, arriving mañana.

Boots are real, contrarians of pixelated worlds. Boots are art.
I reject flipflop falsity, social media, and streamed video sex.

Free at last and always, I return to jake brake concrete and
Fast miles as red dirt takes possession of my mother's vault.

62.

We walk backward on unfurling scrolls. No priests or monks
Can be enlightened, only diesel rig drivers and cowboys.

Kyoto blossoms are falsehoods. Smoke of barbecue shacks
And blood of biker bars mark true nirvana passageways.

Listening to Hank Williams and Lightnin' Hopkins is zazen,
No further practice necessary. I am nothing. You are nothing.

My mother was a human neither good nor bad. I know
I loathed and loved in equal measure with zero sum total.

Faint harmonica in my no light house as north wind blows.
Romantic hopscotch concluded: my gears frozen and done.

63.

Compression blankets too heavy to revoke: I struggle
To breathe. Winter morning light now invades my house

In Texas. I have forsaken too many dawns. This ailment
Is horse crippler cactus. The ensnared list stretches long:

Lincoln/Churchill/Styron/Peckinpah/my mother/grand-
Mother/great grandmother, who dived into Adventist

Madness/great great grandmother who constructed
Permanent night, went to bed and remained decades

In chicken feather dissolution. Boxing, sex, movies kept
Me in motion. Dog walkers begin their rounds outside.

64.

I recall that night in Pasadena, drunk, accepting
Outrageous verbal abuse over Texas telephone

After near collapse beneath L.A. skyline at 1 a.m.
Nothing to do with my mother except everything:

She never knew about this event. She created it.
A couple of miles from where I attempted sleep

The Rose Bowl fell silent. That hillside bedroom
Cost more than all the money I had ever earned.

I listened to bad Mountain music after the call. I slid
Back to eighth grade. Toll lanes are never deserted.

65.

I know two nonbinary women, once lovers, now friends.
Ultramarathons and motherhood are easy fits for them.

One remodels campers and delivers fresh-baked bread.
The other buys chainsaws and massages my worn out

Shoulders. Neither abides shit. They are salvation in this
Dystopian nation, fetterless. I love them both. I see flash

Of censure in my mother's walnut eyes. Outside it is
Ten degrees. Visions of freezing songbirds alarm me.

My mother's years were read 'em and weep. I am sorry.
I strum Kristofferson guitar. Tardy tears wet my beard.

66.

Tonight it is Liz Phair and deceit photos hidden
In my mother's dead closet. No answers here.

I wanted to be Phair's flower. I owned excuses
But no sane explanations, everything lined up

In illusory order. I ponder shaving my beard.
Lo-fi is my natural language. Mom, you never

Absorbed. You mistook loss for deep thought.
I burned tread on Interstates from Texas to

Washington state. People heard you say I was
A star. I am rusted leaf springs, nothing more.

67.

Deceit photo: My mother and another woman
Booth bound with two men at Merl Lindsey's

South Oklahoma City joint, cigarettes behind ears,
Schlitz beer on table, making out at shutter snap,

I have no idea who these other people are. Could
The redneck my mother kisses be my real father?

Without question God created honkytonk angels and
Morning after anguish. Answers are concrete vaulted

And red dirt encrypted. Roadrunners and moles cannot
Liberate them. Graveyards nourish tombstones and lies.

68.

Pump organ and warbled voice: O Mom/Mom/Mom,
No slut-shaming redbuds in blossom — steel guitar

And fiddle yowl — heeding roots deep in copper clay,
Insanity of pleasure and being — we embrace such stains:

Cheesecake pose on '51 Chevy hood, cowboy sugar hugs,
Because we must, our continuance investment, biology,

And because they are Wanda Jackson rockabilly sass.
But Mom/Mom/Mom, you skipped out on breakfast tabs

At South OKC truck stop diners and left me in booths
Alone to deal consequence and sing Neil Young forever.

69.

Killing cold and she is grave snug in Oklahoma.
Single digit thermometers and around me people

Dog huddle in dark, waterless houses. I am secure
And warm. I cannot say why. I remember breakfast

A year ago: I was not a good woman in those days.
I heard her say those words. I owned no response.

I have never been a good man. I disconnect. I hover.
I invest in second-rate directors like Jack Starrett.

I fail the courage and weakness to be Peckinpah.
No sleep, then dawn. Wren carcasses are yard litter.

70.

House my mother no longer needs is my burden.
Record cold in Texas, worse in Oklahoma, no safe

Inoculation at any juncture. Eight inches of snow
And ice at my place. But I have electricity, water,

And gas. I cannot know what survives and perishes,
Except that cypress I planted as a seedling, thirty

Feet tall today and split down the middle, chainsaw
Fodder — it will be that when the melting arrives.

I owe no one explanation or apology for anything.
I live each hour in truth. In frost air I sing with crows.

71.

My mother delivered me into the art of fiction.
My birth certificate is invention. I learned early

Never to trust primary sources. I forgive her.
I trudge out to dawn lit carnage at the end

Of five-day ice age. Clemency never arrives
On skids, nor should it. It is a Nepalian climb.

I bury songbird remains in thawed flower beds.
Honduran men autopsy the cypress then stack it

As firewood. Things expire. Mom never was happy.
Survival birds begin to sing. I stand. I breathe. I see.

72.

Hail damaged my mother's roof a few years ago.
She told me she used insurance to replace it.

She lied. She spent the money on herself. Fine.
It was her windfall. Backhanded truth — I know

That song. Judge's son supplies shingles and nails.
I negotiate from half a thousand miles distant.

Highways are nothing compared to soul fissures.
Again, fine. I carpentered pedestals unclimbable.

Spring defies ice storm death sentence. In shorts
And shirtless I work my yard. This is my penicillin.

73.

Happiness escaped them all, Mom but also stepfather,
Elden, even Dale, whose smiles from last nights and days

Were Mexican dried flower arrangements and cocaine
Warp speed rushes, late 1980s, Fort Worth. At least he

Embraced his queerness before he died, although he
Could not profess it to anyone in red dirt country

Except me. It is April already and I stand in Texas sun.
No song lasts forever: chorus repeated a final time,

Then outro. Pitchfork armed I turn my compost. Even
Agave spikes surrender. I will spread it come October.

74.

John Coltrane and Merle Haggard during 5 a.m. rain.
Nighttime Tao masters pack bags, work complete.

I never supposed I would reach this place. I await
Gutter replacement at dawn once storm subsides.

I still dream Rock Creek in Montana before sleep.
My karma is spinning for muddy water whitefish,

Creel vacant. Mom memory ebbs. No Carolina wrens
Inhabit these trees. A regret: never running into

Peckinpah in Livingston. We arrived at the same time.
I possessed flyrods. He tap-danced death of the West.

75.

Mid-June drive to home I forsook, redbuds, dogwood
Faintly linger ahead of rain front. A nation unmasks

Too soon. As always I fear scaffold collapse and steel
Myself for arrows and shotguns. I park among Native

Plates at Interstate hotel, always the safest place —
No lineage goons or high school branding scars here,

Just antiseptic sheets, shrink-wrap telephones, plastic
Food, forged smiles, white noise machine amity: alone.

Next day convergence with realtor and closing agent
In building afloat on lake. Pen swipes, Mom's house sold.

76.

Sky and lake merge in deluge, title company building
Lost in gray water. Closing papers thrust against skin

Beneath shirt and jacket, I race to my SUV, umbrella
Malfunction, boots sloshing. I retreat to hotel room:

Lightning flash and thunder endless, updates texted,
Poem notions filed. Wet clothes wadded in corner

I lie naked on bed — childhood torture sequences,
Mangled romances, business horrors crowd mind:

I am old, self-discarded, no *High Country* Joel McCrea.
Rains ends. I dress, drive to Whataburger: incomplete.

77.

Dream flash of torched lynching trees — I blink in hotel
Darkness, migraine ascending. Swallowed remedy, then

Predawn run along foreign familiar streets. I once knew
This place. Hot shower, then breakfast at dawn. Headache

Displaced. My mother's house is reduced to largest check
I have possessed. Solitary bird sings. I pack, lug suitcase

To SUV, sunlight in rain scrubbed air. I don Resitol straw
And see John Wayne's J.B. Books in mirror. My steed is

Steel and plastic. I am ready to dispense highwaymen.
Twenty-mile check deposit and at last hobbles crumble.

.

78.

We humans suffer Geomyidae condemnation. We claw caves
And seal ourselves within, breathing our exhalations, touching

Only ourselves, face curve obsessed, sightless beyond our lids,
Darkness content. But I resist in honest sweat daylight. Robert

And I conspire to build morning fence. Opera voice of power
Miter box blade and I am showered in sawdust snow as I cut

Picket after picket, each to fit precisely. Shots from Hitachi
Nail gun become our joint heartbeat. Robert is a sturdy man.

This fence between our properties will bind us. Woodpeckers
And robins celebrate cedar plank nuptials. I sing with them.

79.

Therapy is circular reality TV. We must liberate ourselves.
I remember eating baked grasshoppers in Cimarron sun.

Folded hands of sandstone towered above us. In Texas
I walk barefoot in predawn and wonder if one-button

Rattlesnakes are leaving dens yet. One strike of fire and
Nausea will confirm. It is early summer, too soon for true

Danger. My mother ridiculed my trimmed shrub and flower-
Bed obsession: Ain't no copperheads going to rocket out

To bite you. Oh really? My mother embarrassed me.
She left me ashamed. Asphalt and gravel warm my soles.

80.

Surprise jaunt to Norman and I stand naked at hotel
Window to watch dawn beyond Westheimer Airport.

I no longer hide anything. I am an old man. Last night
I watched *Once Upon a Time in Hollywood* for the

Sixth time, iPad miniaturized. I wish I could re-form
History and romance. I have no issue with flame-

Thrower fricassee of Susan Atkins, evil incarnate:
If only it could have really happened that way.

I grow weary of Princeton ennobled white men
Sporting absurd beards. They have never bled.

81.

My mother never trusted horn-rimmed claques. I concur.
Her reasoning sprouted from populism. Mine from crime:

University department chair said he'd see to it I'd never
Graduate unless I had sex with him. 1970s. I was not alone.

He wound up promoted to dean. Such is university life.
Cedar elm will soon drop leaves. Twenty-third cycle since

I began this particular window gaze. How many more?
I shoved department chair from doorway and released

An unlanded fist. I graduated while he was on sabbatical.
This tree endures. I do too. Morning breaks gold and blue.

82.

I commune with Comanche friends. She refused to do her work:
The end and beginning of everything. I am sorry she was less

Than met the soul. I am not speaking of my mother. I hear voices
Encroach from past legislative halls. It is the sound of betrayal

Then, now, tinnitus unending. Forgiveness vulnerability:
Creaky hand bridge spanning geysers. I have been poached in

Those waters. I salve my skin to this day. I write to the sergeant
At arms. He quit drinking decades ago. We surfed a Kaanapali

Of whiskey during my senate years: the machine's fuel. But now
He is safe, strong, ancient: a totem. I feel equinox approaching.

83.

Mother, I drive to you a final time, legal decree in hand.
Our family life is liquified, ready for disbursement. Last

Safe deposit box is surrendered: It held only Grandpa's
Faded paper bones: military exemption, Social Security

Filings. Why did you cling to such things? It was your way,
I understand that: I had to root through your house like

A feral hog. Living room filled to ceiling with trash bags
And repurposed boxes. *It was your way. . .* But everything

Is clean now, house sold, squalor vanquished. Grave visit
In clean June light. I did the best I could. Moles are at work.

84.

Mother, my secret ledger is thick. I invested too much
Into lust and poetry, too late to retrieve that currency.

You taught me clandestine life. I lived six decades before
I began to balance my books in sunlight. Your time was

Layered with guile and Yuban coffee cans filled with
Pennies and half dollars hidden in closets I never knew.

I open my accounts payable book and lay it on cemetery
Grass. I do not care who reads it. Roadrunners and moles

Peer at pages beyond your tombstone. This is how I love
And breathe these days. I touch your clean stone numbers.

85.

Mother, I am a movie cowboy named Jack Burns
And I ride a horse called Whiskey through this

Technology nightmare. I understand our demise
Will be Archie Bunker driving a semi-trailer truck

Loaded with toilets. I am sorry you inserted your
Purpose into the gaze of a man with broken eyes.

I bled and I carry scars. I learned no one can lean
On family or anyone else. It comes down to what

We see with our own eyes. I spread the blanket
On Whiskey. He snorts at the saddle. It is the way.

86.

Mother, I am Warren Oates chasing Warren Oates
Across Kanab badlands. The film has no point and

That is precisely the point. I lived Western violence.
I photographed so many murdered men and women

Against bleeding Oklahoma nights: two a.m. phone
Calls when I lived at your house. I'd depart loaded

With Kodak Tri-X and Smith & Wesson. Do you recall?
It was flies crawling on Leone faces. It was Peckinpah

Anguish and filth. Only more so. No Star Wars spic-and-
Span. I was not even 20. Those bodies share your soil.

87.

Mother, I cannot pledge I will visit your grave again.
I know you were a teenage Mariette Hartley trapped

In Hammond brother terror. You were an innocent.
No Joel McCrea stepped in to rescue you. Grandpa

Had too much R.G. Armstrong in his soul. You violated
Code and Good Book in his eyes. I believe you fell prey to

Date rape, then blame and shame where compassion
Was discarded peanut shells and snuff spit. I am sorry

For all you suffered. I'm also sorry you embraced deceit
And mentholated cigarettes to get by, all words snuffed.

88.

Mother, morning presses on. I must soon take leave.
I recollect when earthquakes hit the old place. Never

In my time there did we have them. But then they came
Almost daily: oil field salt-water high-pressure injection,

Different from my rig days. I remember when the old man
Lost his body and spent days dying in living room chairs.

Squirrels and rats gnawed their way into your dream house,
Fouling shag carpet and black velvet painting alike. I was

Disconnected and could not help, a dolphin trapped in tuna
Netting. I gave you thousands then sank in dead Gulf water.

89.

Mother, I understand this land forged me. I look around.
Nothing resonates, not even scenes from strong 1930s

Movies. I see houses I have known forever beyond graves.
They are foreign addresses now. Insects of myth crawl.

They bite my back and thighs. The sheriff is disappointed
I never fed you horse dewormer, sure thing cancer cure.

I cannot own this place. Maybe I am Charles Floyd bristling
At being called Pretty Boy. Maybe I am the dung beetles

At work near an 1893 grave. I am lost in these locales
Because I know them too well. Goodbye, Mom. Goodbye.

90.

I roll from cemetery to old-new bank whose name
Changes with each Cottonwood flood. Elden awaits.

We walk inside and speculate about offices of men
Who died before new millennium. Nothing lingers.

I feel close to him, only time in our lives. We endure.
Kind woman behind plexiglass divides all that remains

Of my parents' lives into two checks. Sun warms brick
Streets outside. We pose for photo, first time ever,

Just the two of us framed, doubtful we will see
Each other again. He departs: white truck, red dirt.

91.

Bank of America check deposit in Edmond,
I am masked like Dalton Brothers as I enter,

Resistol low on my brow: Such are our times.
VP approves transaction. I would have emptied

The till in earlier life, shotgun elbow crooked,
Then fled on paint across red dirt prairieland.

Now: just another uncalloused suburbanite
Content to toe line and sign where requested.

Papers in hand, I hat tip Grat Dalton, who blows
Morning cut grass outside. Moon dies bloodless.

92.

Strip malls and fast-food glitter, then university
Sprawl — I know this place, it is foreign to me.

Liberal arts bricks, ancient now, cutting edge then,
Times of revelation and crime. Nothing to see here —

Forgive holstered dreams, drive on, turnpikes with
Unknown names, extended broad ways, surviving

Is the true miracle — I am Phaedrus streaming
Hank Williams and Patsy Cline in morning sun

While wearing 1970s hat and jeans, all claims
Discharged. I can depart this territory at last.

93.

Lexus dissolve to 1975 BWM R75/5, four-lanes
Headed southwest — the best — OKC sprawl

Fading behind me, motorcycle wheels holy
On H.E. Bailey concrete, luggage trashed

At truckstop receptacle twenty miles behind.
I am a pilgrim frantic for shrines. I know

Where they lie. This is no movie. Billy Sims
Barbecue break in Wichita Mountain loom:

I am where this began: *rocks sweat mists,*
Vultures kettle. Forty years ago. Noon sings.

94.

In midst of Wichita Mountain granite, Army post entry:
I am passage-granted. I ride in accordance along military

Roads toward artillery range and Beef Creek. I have not
Known more peace than at this place, here, surrounded

By warfare practice. Trees waited forty years for my return.
I sacrificed much for suburb intrigue and lust. I waltz BWM

Into shade pool. Leaves are silent pending detection.
Then: symphonic rustle like ten thousand rattlesnakes.

It is good to be home. I approach Geronimo in his grave.
I touch his stone name. I knew this way once but frayed it.

95.

My mother owned no vision or wind. I regret that.
I stand among markers. Warriors, prophets, healers,

Wives, husbands, diplomats surround me. I study
Granite mounds and their secrets and think about

Peckinpah far removed from L.A. He touched Tao paths
With a Basque immigrant hundreds of miles from celluloid

Hollywood lion traps. He listened to soundless music
From clean dessert rocks: santua. The apaiz brewed

Coffee, nodded, and spoke of high-country sheep. Yes.
I bid Sam and Geronimo adieu and depart Beef Creek.

96.

Motorcycle miles across cotton fields and ranches:
Once prime buffalo, coyote, antelope, wolf range,

Now center-pivot anointed and betrayed. I cross
Red River, drover in reverse. This plain is my hope.

Deposited in highway hotel, new in 1983, untouched
Through trailing decades, I remove old eyes, recline

On bed bug protection. Everything is forecast. I know
Yet cannot know what awaits me. I do my best to sleep.

I recollect: Beauty seen as beauty is ugliness. Dirt and
Redberry cedar are inglorious glory. Smooth slumber.

97.

New eyes, nap grogged, I ride away toward
Medicine Mounds, unsure and sure at once.

Roaring down ranch road I spy caliche trail.
It seizes me. Yanked from asphalt comfort,

White mother buried far behind, I navigate
Rut and rock to clearing on the big mound:

Teepee rises against bleeding sunset.
First thing: I see Roadman tell diamondback

It must depart. No coil threat, snake complies
And spreads rattled word to its brothers.

98.

Unlined teepee orange in snakeless night:
I enter with respect and thanks. Comanche

Songs unheard yet known — water drum
Fast and clean, guard rattle harmony,

Half-moon altar and green tobacco, buttons,
Tea. For once gopher eyes and claws fall

Away. I am unconfined by earthen tubes.
Full-sighted, I trace peyote road sands.

Quanah's great grandson tells me some
Lyrics possess mystery meaning. I sing.

99.

Next night, I return to same clearing. Buffalo
Hides and green willow displace teepee glow,

Firepit of oak, Cache Creek granite cantaloupe.
Milky way clear overhead, I enter sweat lodge

With seven young Comanche, one young Kiowa.
Bowmaker leads us. He directs igneous placement.

Heat overwhelms yet comforts. I douse myself
With spring water from buffalo horn: holy rite.

I hear prayers and songs from young Native men
In red rock radiance. Everything ends/begins here.

100.

Dawn blessing of cedar smoke and sage whisk
Surrounded by rattlesnake shade. We are freed.

I am sweat-cleansed as I make sky island climb.
Light triumphs on flat Medicine Mound summit.

White moon death behind. Turquoise birth ahead.
Circle of horizon, Wichita Mountains showcased

To the northeast, a hundred miles away yet here,
Ghosts and bones of Quanah and Geronimo

Welded to this and every rock. I know reckoning.
I squat, scoop dirt and roots, and face the wind

www.ingramcontent.com/pod-product-compliance
Lightning Source LLC
Chambersburg PA
CBHW021508090426
42739CB00007B/515